F IN

RETAKES

F IN RETAKES

Summersdale Publishers Ltd
46 West Street
Chichester
West Sussex
PO19 1RP
UK

www.summersdale.com

Printed and bound by CPI Group (UK) Ltd, Croydon, CR0 4YY

ISBN: 978-1-84953-313-3

Substantial discounts on bulk quantities of Summersdale books are available to corporations, professional associations and other organisations. For details telephone Summersdale Publishers on (+44-1243-771107), fax (+44-1243-786300) or email (nicky@summersdale.com).

F IN RETAKES

EVEN MORE TEST PAPER BLUNDERS

Richard Benson

summersdale

Contents

Introduction

Remember when school was out, the sun was out and your friends were out – but you were stuck in the classroom slaving over past papers? You wanted to be enjoying your summer but your parents had you chained to the desk and you weren't allowed to come down until you'd memorised the entire works of Shakespeare and some algebra too. At the time you may have thought you were the only one whose summer holiday was a sweaty nightmare of revision and more revision but you weren't alone – plenty of people have suffered through the pain of retakes.

Following on from the bestselling *F in Exams*, these students may not have known what they were talking about the first time around but they're back – and they still can't get it right! Loaded with loopy laughs and magnificently funny misunderstandings, you'll find yourself snickering at Shakespeare, snorting at sums and doubling over with laughter at Drama.

Thank goodness school's out for you!

Subject: ...Science...........................

Give two examples of things that plants compete for.

Best smell award.
Biggest flower award.

Harry would like to test the rate at which sugar is converted into energy in the human body. What equipment does he need?

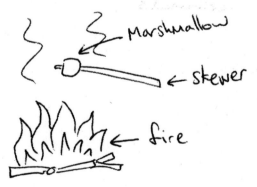

What is meant by non-biodegradable?

Washing powder.

What might purified copper be used for?

Catching purified criminals

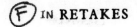

How are vegetable oils hydrogenated?

With ease

What evidence is there to suggest that the Earth far exceeds the age of 400 million years?

It's WRINKLY WITH MOUNTAINS AND CANYONS

What damaging effects does sulphur dioxide inflict on the environment?

It smells horrible

Why would carbon dioxide not be emitted from a wind-powered generator?

Because wind -powered generators are all-inclusive.

Describe energy produced by the human body.

Nervous energy.

What does a beta particle consist of?

Improved substances.

Yo!

What conclusions can be drawn about the universe from red-shift?

It's becoming more left-wing.

Which organisms cause the decay of leaves?

Humans, when they stamp on them.

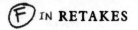

What is an antibiotic used for?

To stop people being biotic.

Name an example of a biofuel.

Manure.

Subject: **Sociology**

What is meant by gender socialisation?

When people only go
places with the same
gender - boys + boys,
girls + girls

What would be one way of selecting a sample of
school children? What would be the advantages and
disadvantages of this method?

Choosing the tallest ones.
No disadvantages -
they all have a better
vantage point.

What do sociologists mean by the term 'the hidden curriculum'?

When the teacher loses their lesson plan.

What is meant by 'domestic roles'?

An actor who gets typecast as a cleaner

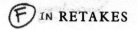

Give one reason why a university student would work and study at the same time.

BECAUSE STUDYING ON ITS OWN IS REALLY BORING.

How would a child's education be affected by growing up in poverty?

They would learn how to bargain hunt.

Sociology

Give one reason why someone would not vote in a general election.

THEY MIGHT ONLY WANT TO VOTE IN A SPECIFIC ELECTION

Name two methods the general public can use to influence government policy.

1. Voting in an election.

2. Blowing up houses of parliament.

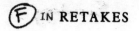

What is functionalist theory?

The opposite of dysfunctionalist theory.

What is a disadvantage of using official statistics?

You can't make things up.

What happens at the operationalisation stage of the research process?

The surgeons get to work.

What is meant by the term fieldwork?

IT IS WHAT THE PEOPLE WHO CAN'T BAT OR BOWL DO IN ROUNDERS

What sources are there for social and ethnic stereotypes?

Tomato ketchup in the South,
brown sauce in the North.

What are the main components of Marxist beliefs?

They like the Marx brothers,
who were in films.

Sociology

What overlap is there between the beliefs of Feminism and Marxism?

ism.

In sociology, what does Action theory state?

No matter how many baddies are shooting at him, the hero never dies

Give an example of a social norm?

Having coffee with friends

Argue for one side of the nature vs nurture debate.

↗

I argue for this side

Sociology

State a social value that differs greatly in two cultures.

£1

Discuss the changing nature of social class.

It changes every year as we get older e.g. we'll be in year 8 next year.

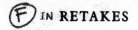

What is social closure?

When the local pub has a
lock in.

What is meant by the term social role?

Bread that is often seen
out and about.

What are the key features of Weberian theory?

What significance does differential achievement have in the UK educational system?

It's different for different people

Give an example of a primary source. Explain why it is
a primary source.

TOMATO SOURCE BECAUSE
NEARLY EVERYONE LOVES
IT

How does Neo-Marxism differ from Marxism?

Its followers all
wear brightly
coloured clothes.

Subject: **Music**

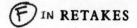

What is meant by the term a cappella?

A smaller than normal hat.

Give an example of a song cycle in classical music.

'There are 9 million bicycles in Beijing' by Katie Melua

What are the main features of baroque music?

It can't be fixed.

Give an example of a sonata. What makes your example a sonata?

Frank Sonata. He was a born Sonata.

What are the components of a diminished seventh chord?

Fewer than the
components of a
whole seventh chord

What are the four groups of an orchestra?

Drums, strings, wood and
wind.

What is a fugue?

Someone who is on the run from the police.

Explain the chromatic scale and give an example of its use in music.

The chromatic scale is a brightly coloured scale measuring everything from red through to purple

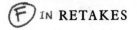

In music terms, what is a vamp?

Are you telling me there's a Twilight musical? OMG

When a score instructs you to play an arpeggio, what does this mean?

It's getting a bit too big for its boots.

What are the key differences between a waltz and a march?

A waltz is a type of dance. A march is what soldiers do.

What is the Italian term for a change of speed in music?

Fast-a, fast-a

What is the effect of a change of key?

New locks

What is ground bass?

GRINDED UP FISH

Explain the idea of homophony.

A cake house.

What are the main features of a Scots ballad?

Indistinguishable lyrics.

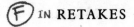

How does a mezzo soprano differ from a soprano?

One has cheese on it.

How would you recognise a walking bass?

Music

Explain what a pentatonic scale is and give an example of its use.

It is an instrument used in devil worship.

What is pizzicato?

Part of an Italian cat.

Define the term 'atonal'.

Something that
goes on forever.

Give examples of instruments you would find in the percussion section of an orchestra.

Blunt instruments.

What are the benefits of an ensemble over a solo performer?

If one's really bad, the others can cover it up.

What is a leitmotiv?

The opposite of a heavy motive.

Subject: .....Economics.....

Economics

Explain a reason why a railway provider would shut down a rural railway line.

A track invasion by cows.

Describe trends in passenger numbers using UK airports.

At the moment there are lots of florals and pastel colours

What effects would a speed limit have on a small town?

More people would have points on their licenses.

How could a country decrease the import of foreign goods?

By not importing them

Economics

Using supply and demand, explain the increase in the price of petrol.

PETROL STATION OWNERS
DEMAND THAT DRIVERS
SUPPLY THEM WITH MORE
MONEY

In what ways are monopolies a negative thing for consumers?

It's really boring and takes about 8 hours to finish a game.

In economic terms, what is meant by the supply of something being perfectly inelastic?

It's not made of elastic.

What is meant by the term 'negative equity'?

A miserable horse.

What happens when an economy is experiencing inflation?

It gets blown up.

What advantages and disadvantages does the market domination of supermarkets have for consumers?

Advantage – All the markets are now super.

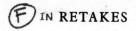

In what ways could the Government make British industry more competitive worldwide?

Put P.E teachers in charge of it.

What is meant by the term 'fiscal policy'?

Where along a river you are allowed to fish

What is one way of measuring a business's performance?

How many followers they
have on Twitter

What effects would a fall in the rate of interest have on businesses?

With less interest, less people
will take up business.

What does the term 'economies of scale' mean?

When people use alternatives to money i.e. shells or scales.

What is meant by the term 'subsidy'?

When something, for example a house, sinks into the ground.

Economics

What problems can be caused by rising unemployment?

Increased addictions to daytime t.v.

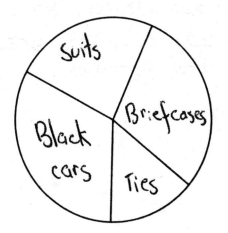

Complete the pie chart to show how a government minister might organise spending.

Suits

Briefcases

Black cars

Ties

Subject: ....ICT...............

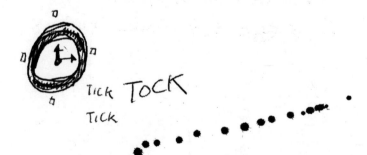

TICK TOCK
TICK

ICT

Give two examples of computer input devices and what they are used for.

Left hand and right hand.

What does CAD stand for and what is a CAD package used for?

A CAD stands for dishonourable behaviour and uses his package for rude things.

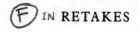

What other types of keyboard are there?

Musical keyboard.

What is the difference between a LAN and a WAN?

A WAN is paler.

ICT

What is OCR?

A SORT OF YELLOWISH COLOUR

How does ROM function differently to RAM?

It's less violent than RAM.

What are the main functions of an operating system?

It organises all the doctors so that operations can take place.

Give an example of when it would be useful to use a database's 'sort data' function?

When your data is getting all in your face and needs sorting out.

Where is data stored on a swipe card?

In your wallet
or purse.

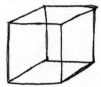

What input device would be used for transferring an image on paper onto a computer?

Tracing paper

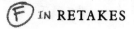

What sort of program would you use to do a mail merge?

I'd put something boring on so not to distract me from sorting all the envelopes

What is a GUI?

The opposite to a girl.

What is a disadvantage of video conferencing against face-to-face meetings?

You get lonely.

What methods should be used to ensure a password is secure?

Write it on some paper and tape it firmly to the desk.

TOP SECRET

password 1
password
password 1 !

What risks can an Internet connection have to data stored on a computer?

The internet is always at risk of distracting people from work.

What is an appropriate way of storing back-up copies of photographs?

In a photo album.

Define the terms 'software' and 'hardware'.

It's like a floppy disk vs. a hard disk.

What is hexadecimal and what is it used for?

When you put a curse on maths.

Subject: English

How does Dylan Thomas use voices to create an image of village life in Wales?

Putting on accents when he reads it out loud.

How are the mountain range's conditions described in *Touching the Void*?

THE MOUNTAINS ARE PORTRAYED AS BEING HIGH AND POINTY, WITH SOME SNOWY PARTS AND SOME NOT SO

Describe the differences in character between Macbeth and Lady Macbeth.

They are the same but one is a female version.

Do you think Heathcliff is an angry character? How has Brontë's writing influenced your opinion?

Bronte invented Heathcliff, which is how she made us think he was angry.

Give two conventions of a screenplay.

The California Screenplay Convention 1990. The London Screenplay Convention.

What would you say was the key theme of *The Prime of Miss Jean Brodie*?

Maths and female mathematicians.

In what sort of writing would it be appropriate to use bullet points?

Aggressive writing.

When would a dash be used?

When you're in a rush.

When might you use inverted commas?

When you're reading
upside down.

In what circumstances would you employ a semicolon?

When they have a
good c.v. and
interview.

What are pronouns?

People in favour of nouns

Which sentence is correct?

a) Please tell Damien if there are less than five books in the library.

b) Please tell Damien if there are fewer than five books in the library.

Neither, libraries should always have more than five books.

Subject: .... *Psychology* ....

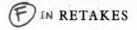
What are the benefits of participant observation?

Great, if you are nosy.

What is event sampling?

Going to lots of events to
see what they're like

Psychology

How easily influenced is eyewitness testimony?

very easily, with money
and intimidation.

What is an EEG and what is it used for?

It's a food used for scrambling
in cooked breakfasts or cold in
sandwiches.

In what ways do psychological tests on animals lack validity?

THEY'RE RUBBISH BECAUSE
ANIMALS CAN'T WRITE
THEIR OWN ANSWERS

How can quantitative data be more useful than qualitative?

There is more of it.

What assumptions does the developmental approach make?

That you will develop
mental problems eventually.

What strengths does the psychodynamic approach have?

DYNAMISM

How effective have media campaigns been shown to be in relation to the promotion of health?

Chocolate bars have really good adverts so obesity goes up.

How reliable are the methods of measuring stress?

Not very – if you're stressed you'll probably not take very accurate measurements.

Outline the Oedipus complex.

What can MRI scans be used to measure?

The length of an MRI

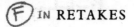

Explain a psychological technique for managing stress.

Punching your pillow

How can a study avoid being affected by individual differences?

ASK THE SAME PERSON
100 TIMES

What is a dependent variable?

One that can't be left alone.

What problems are there with the self-report method of data collection?

People are liars.

What benefits are there to using a closed-question survey rather than one with open questions?

Yes.

What ethical issues might arise regarding an experiment involving children?

Children can't be trusted.

Psychology

What is a snapshot study?

When you examine a photograph.

What does 'diffusion of responsibility' mean?

Giving your work to someone else.

Subject: Drama

What is the importance of the performer in modern theatre?

It would be a really boring Play without any actors.

Discuss the effect of theatre technology in one contemporary piece.

Robots aren't very emotive

Analyse the role of the director in modern theatre.

THE ROLE OF THE DIRECTOR
IS TO DIRECT, LIKE THE ROLE
OF THE ACTOR IS TO ACT

What effect do the comic characters in Shakespeare's non-comic plays have?

They ruin the mood.

Drama

What elements of a play could be evaluated and developed as it is created?

The bad bits.

Give an example of an effective use of staging.

Successfully building a stage.

Ezzzzzz...

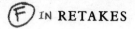

Discuss what is most important out of lighting, sound and costume.

Costume, unless it is a nudist play.

In stage lighting, what is gel?

A slimy substance.

What is meant by the terms 'protagonist' and 'antagonist'?

A protagonist is for agonists and an antagonist is against them

What elements should be included in a stage ground plan?

A stage, the ground.

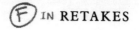

What is a monologue?

When one person won't shut up.

Give an example of a way body language can be used to portray emotion.

Putting your fingers up at somebody when you are annoyed.

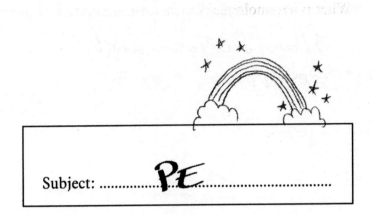

Subject: ......PE.........................

Name ONE factor that will increase sports participation.

Increased sports.

What national facilities does Sport England run?

Sports facilities.

What will concessions mean for some groups at sports facilities?

Admitting defeat.

Name a common advantage for a country hosting a world sporting event.

They can stay at their own houses

What aspect of Rugby League changed in order to meet the needs of television?

Everyone got their hair done

What pressure resulted in the introduction of the tie-break in tennis?

FROM PLAYERS PULLING ON THE UMPIRE'S TIE TOO HARD

What influences can encourage good sporting behaviour amongst young people?

Scary P.E. teachers.

What name is given to an unpaid participant in sport?

Slave.

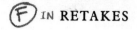

How often are the Olympic games held?

Every 400 years.

What is the name given to the physical activity which improves health and fitness?

Playing the Wii.

What sport requires flexibility?

Limbo dancing.

What is the purpose rules serve in sport?

They make sure the lines at the edges of the pitches are straight.

In cricket, what is referred to as a 'delayed dead ball'?

Someone reacting slowly to
being hit in the crotch.

What factors can make a competition balanced?

Holding your arms out straight
and staring at a spot on the wall.

What must sportspeople do before taking part in a sports activity?

Get to where the sports activity is taking place

What skill is required by sprinters?

Big legs.

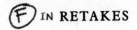

What qualities does a good referee possess?

A strong whistle.

Who plans the strategies for a team?

Mr~~T~~ Hannibal

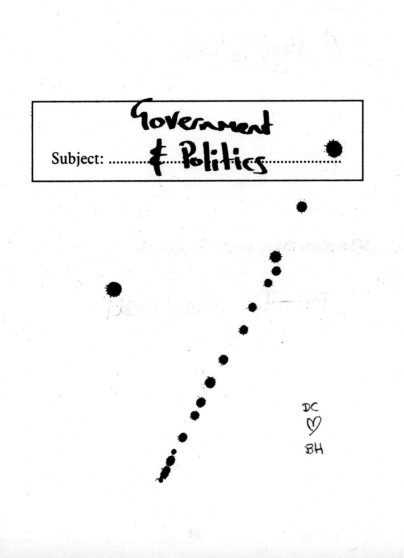

Subject: ......**Government & Politics**......

DC
♡
BH

Why do some people participate in democracy more than others?

Because only some people are politicians.

What is a nation-state?

A country that's in a bad state.

Why might global corporations be considered more powerful than governments?

THEY OWN THE GLOBE WHEREAS GOVERNMENTS OWN COUNTRIES

What is meant by the term 'federal' state?

A place where everyone has to wear a hat.

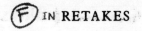

What are the benefits of a pluralist democracy?

Two heads are better than one!

What is the difference between the executive and the legislature?

The executive runs the company, the legislature is the rules.

What beliefs are common to those who are classed as Eurosceptics?

They don't think
Europe exists.

Explain the meaning of the term 'sovereignty'.

When you drop a ring in your tea.

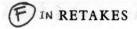

What part does the House of Lords play in legislative procedure?

IT KEEPS THE PEOPLE INVOLVED IN THE PROCEDURE WARM AND DRY.

What effect does devolution have on the way the UK is governed?

It means it's governed by Monkeys!

In US politics, what does the term 'impeachment' mean?

It's like imprisonment, but with fruit.

In what way does the US constitution restrict the government's actions?

THEY HAVE A WEAK CONSTITUTION AND SO CAN'T TAKE MUCH EXERCISE

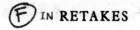

If a government is given a mandate, what does this mean? How might this come about?

A mandate is a boys' night out. A womandate is a girls' night out.

What caused the increase in labour mobility within the EU?

More exercise.

What changes would a codified UK constitution bring about?

More people eating cod.

What effect does a strong judiciary have on civil liberties?

Judiciary overpowers liberties, because they are too polite.

Explain the relationship between the US Senate, House of Representatives and the president.

They get on really well.

What government policies would be considered to assist or hinder multiculturalism?

Assist: helpful policies
Hinder: Unhelpful policies.

Outline the basic difference between left-wing and right-wing political beliefs.

It's all about which side you're sat on.

In what ways is the 'first past the post' electoral system undemocratic?

It's not fair to people who can't run very fast

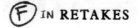

What arguments are used against international aid?

IT'S NOT AS NICE AS CHERRYADE

Who sits in the Council of the European Union?

Saruman.

Subject: **Media Studies**

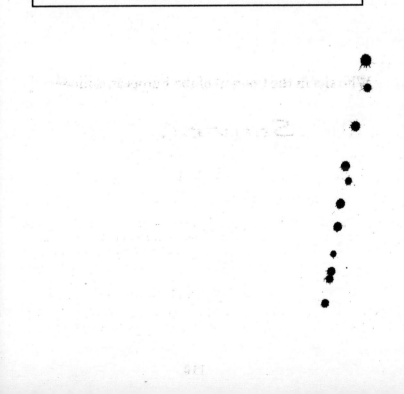

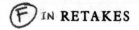

What types of media need to be suited to a wide demographic?

TV, 'cause our sofa's really long.

How can television provide a public service?

Showing less reality shows

How has the nature of magazine publication changed in the past 30 years?

There is less nature to publish photos of because of global warming.

How are television advertisements aimed at their target audience?

Through the screen.

How have representations of young people changed in the news over time?

They've got older and been replaced

How does layout design affect the way publications are viewed?

If your newspaper is bigger than you, you are viewed as posh

What elements of a film poster can be used to attract potential viewers' attention?

BOLD LETTERING!

How can a soundtrack affect the mood of a film clip?

Depends what the soundtrack says to the film clip.

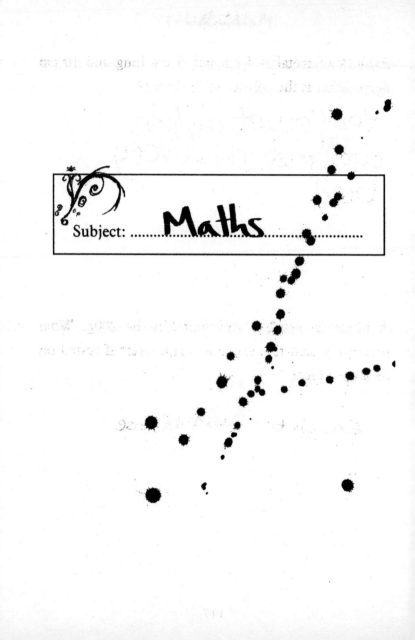

Subject: ....Maths.................

A block of metal is 4 cm tall, 5 cm long and 10 cm deep. What is the volume of the block?

Very quiet, unless dropped. Then very loud.

A block is weighed and found to be 200g. What pressure would this size and shape exert if rested on its largest face?

Enough to squash its nose.

Calculate the mean of this group of numbers:

2, 12, 5, 8, 4, 19, 8

Eight looks quite mean.

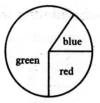

The diagram shows a fair spinner.

Which colour is the arrow least likely to land on?

Yellow

Maths

A hat costs £5 in the UK.
The same hat in Germany costs €8.00
The exchange rate is £1 = €1.40
Where would be cheaper to buy the hat from?

Taking the plane fare into account, the UK.

Give a two-digit square number smaller than 70.

47

If tickets to a football match cost £12.50 each, how much would it cost for Johnny and his three brothers to go.

£12.50 each

Lisa wants to knit two types of jumper, one requiring 2½ balls of wool and one requiring 1¾ balls, using only 4 balls of wool. Can she do it?

Only if she can actually knit.

James' monthly outgoing costs are £50 on his mobile phone, £80 on utilities, £450 on rent and £80 on savings. Draw and label a pie chart to represent his outgoing costs.

Oscar has three orange cards and nine green cards. What is the probability he picks a blue card?

9/12 if he's colour blind.

A town has a population of 80,000 to the nearest ten thousand.

What is the greatest possible population?

It depends on their combined achievements.

Samuel gets £15 a week for doing his chores. His parents increase this by £2 on his fourteenth birthday. What does he get after this?

A gambling problem.

A train that normally travels at an average of 60 mph leaves 30 minutes late. If it increases its average speed to 65 mph will it be on time?

No, trains are never on time.

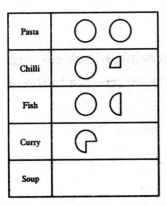

This pictogram shows the school lunches for the week.

Key: ◯ = 4 lunches

How many times was curry eaten in the week?

Pac-Man!

Ciara says that if she spins a spinner with an equal chance of landing on white, red, blue or green fifty times it will land on green four times. Is she correct? Explain your answer.

No.

Because Ciara is an idiot.

Draw a stem-and-leaf diagram to show the number of cups of tea consumed by a surveyed group of offices in a week:

46 12 4 83 25 9 60 42 34 36 19

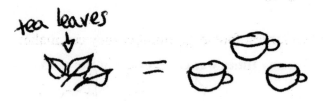

tea leaves

Maths

What are moving averages used for?

Maths on the go.

4 9 3 5

Use these digits to create:

a) The smallest four-digit number they can make:

4935

b) The largest four-digit number they can make:

4 9 3 5

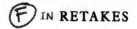

Write 7834 in words.

SEVEN EIGHT THREE FOUR

mmm

Draw a tetrahedron.

If you're interested in finding out more about our humour books, follow us on Twitter: @SummersdaleLOL

www.summersdale.com